# YOUR KNOWLEDGE HAS VALUE

- We will publish your bachelor's and master's thesis, essays and papers

- Your own eBook and book - sold worldwide in all relevant shops

- Earn money with each sale

## Upload your text at www.GRIN.com and publish for free

Erica Thompson

# An Investigation of Aggression and Bullying in the Workplace

GRIN Verlag

**Bibliografische Information der Deutschen Nationalbibliothek:**

Die Deutsche Bibliothek verzeichnet diese Publikation in der Deutschen National-
bibliografie; detaillierte bibliografische Daten sind im Internet über http://dnb.d-
nb.de/ abrufbar.

**Imprint:**

Copyright © 2011 GRIN Verlag GmbH
Druck und Bindung: Books on Demand GmbH, Norderstedt Germany
ISBN: 978-3-656-25958-9

**This book at GRIN:**

http://www.grin.com/en/e-book/199344/an-investigation-of-aggression-and-bullying-
in-the-workplace

## GRIN - Your knowledge has value

Der GRIN Verlag publiziert seit 1998 wissenschaftliche Arbeiten von Studenten, Hochschullehrern und anderen Akademikern als eBook und gedrucktes Buch. Die Verlagswebsite www.grin.com ist die ideale Plattform zur Veröffentlichung von Hausarbeiten, Abschlussarbeiten, wissenschaftlichen Aufsätzen, Dissertationen und Fachbüchern.

**Visit us on the internet:**

http://www.grin.com/

http://www.facebook.com/grincom

http://www.twitter.com/grin_com

An Investigation of Aggression and Bullying in the Workplace

Dissertation Paper

In Partial Fulfillment of the
Requirements for the Degree of

DOCTOR OF PHILOSOPHY

by

Erica Renita Thompson

Dedicated to my parents: Doris & George Thompson

Table of Contents

## Introduction

Bullying behavior at work is much more rampant than previously thought even though such behavior is a frequently overlooked area of concern (Agervold, 2007). Aggression and violence including verbal or physical abuse bear enormous costs for employers, workers, and the health and mental care sectors. Enterprises worried about sustainable competitiveness in an age of globalize business rivalry count no cost excessive when it comes to acquiring equipment and implementing processes that will raise staff productivity; however, many companies do not appear to address the immense negative impact of bullying behavior on workers. Efforts by researchers to define bullying in the workplace have yet to provide enough insight to solve the problem (Agervold, 2007; Kelly, 2006; Khalil, 2009; Lally, 2009; Minton & Minton, 2004; Privitera & Campbell, 2009; Randle & Stevenson, 2007; Simon & Simon, 2006; Yildirim, 2007; Yildiz, 2007).

The study of bullying in the workplace commenced as a special interest in the studies of Heinz Leymann in the 1980s (as cited in Yildiz, 2007). Meanwhile Adams (1990), who also studied workplace bullying, claimed that only a few recognized that it could take place "between adults outside of the confines of a schoolyard" (as cited in Randle & Stevenson, 2007, p. 49). While awareness grew regarding rights and protections for specific groups (e.g. minorities, the physically handicapped, women), occupational health regulations do not explicitly foster oversight for bullying and physical harassment in the workplace, which is often aggravated by an increasingly diverse workforce.

## Problem Statement

Bullying at the workplace merits concern for many reasons, including: (a) the detrimental effects on teamwork, (b) low morale, (c) focus on workplace goals, (d) organizational cohesiveness, (e) productivity and quality drives, and (f) turnover of trained staff. Bullying also impels victims to seek counseling, and they may require medical care when aggravated assault is involved.

The phenomenon of hidden bullying in the workplace is a critical psychological and behavioral issue; however, organizations lack awareness, become tolerant, or are negligent of the immense negative impact of bullying workers. Research (e.g., Anderson & Bushman, 2002) in human aggression document the effect-danger ratio in that aggressive adults seek to maximize harm to others by minimizing danger to themselves. Thus the dynamic functioning of the effect-danger ratio may suggest that covert aggression may be more common than overt aggression in the workplace.

Covert bullying in the workplace may be more prevalent than previously acknowledged in existing literature. In the United States of America alone, more than 37% of American workers claim to have been bullied at one time or another in the past (Workplace Bullying Institute, 2007). In addition, the changing complexion of occupations in America with white-collar services supplanting agriculture and manufacturing in importance merely seems to have transferred the context for sustained and hurtful bullying.

The psychological impact of workplace bullying has far-reaching implications for parents, schools, and employers. The theoretical perspective of social constructivism is an appropriate paradigm to examine how individuals seek understanding of the world in which they live and work (Creswell, 2009) and in the particular to allow some degree of objectivity in understanding the cause and patterns of behavior workplace bullying. Social constructivism is premised upon the assumption that those involved in a phenomenon have valid observations. In the occurrence of workplace bullying, both the person (s) enacting bullying behaviors and the victim of bullying behaviors have valid observations that may delineate further the phenomenon of workplace bullying

The proposed study will make sense of (or interpret) the meanings others have about the world by taking their subjective experiences of abusive parenting and/or bullying and viewing it through a more objective lens (for example, developing a list of psychological attributes most commonly associated with workplace bullying based on participants' responses). While the stories and experiences themselves may be highly subjective, the researcher can use research, comparative statistics, and other objective means, as well as the researcher's own analysis to make this study highly applicable to other cases, thereby raising the understanding of this behavior and clarify the role of the effect - ratio dynamic as it relates to aggression theory in the workplace.

**Purpose of the Study**

The aim of this study is to derive insight into the characteristics of bullying perpetrators and victims in the workplace. The researcher will profile the socio-demographic and organizational status of those who repeatedly engage in bullying in order to uncover the personality traits relevant to such aggressive behavior. Similarly, the researcher will profile the demographic characteristics, personality traits, and organizational position of the bully-victims. The study is designed to address significant gaps in the body of knowledge by:

1) Investigating the current prevalence of workplace bullying by the type of workplace in a given metropolitan area, Fort Lauderdale, Florida.

2) Defining character traits, socio-demographic profile, and family-life antecedents that characterize perpetrators and victims (see definition of terms) of workplace bullies.

With respect to antecedents, the study will focus on the possible role of dysfunctional upbringing, the present home life, and prominent traits of workplace bullies. Given the stage of inquiry in this field, and looking to replicate findings on prevalence while being open to unique features of local organizations; the research design will employ the mixed methods research model. The rationale for mixed methods design (Trochim & Donnelly, 2008) consists partly of the stage at which the research is taking place, especially in relation to prior work in the field. Next, there is the matter of whether the qualitative research component informs subsequent quantitative-type research or runs on parallel tracks with the latter.

Since previous studies merely engaged in meta-analysis or pure mathematical modeling of personality profiling, both of which are exclusively quantitative techniques, the mixed method approach will provide greater insight in investigating the phenomenon of hidden bullying in the workplace. This research design will holistically explore and describe the prevalence of bullying in different work settings. Furthermore, this approach will be useful in investigating the aspect of dysfunctional upbringing, as well as the prominent traits of workplace bullies. The mixed method approach will allow the researcher to gain a deeper understanding about the complex nature of bullying at the workplace.

**Research Questions**

The research questions for my proposed study are:

*Q1*: What is the self-reported incidence of perpetrating bullying treatment in the workplace?

*Q2*: How does the prevalence of bullying differ by type of work setting?

*Q3*: What are the self-reported traits and dysfunctional aspects of upbringing and present family life that are distinctive of bullying perpetrators?

*Q4:*     How do department heads and human resource managers respond to bullying in

the workplace?

*Q5:*     Is hierarchical, peer, or upward bullying more prevalent and does overt aggression

really reflect inadequacy?

The aforementioned research questions will guide the choice of study participants,

interview questions, and general approach to this subject area. For the given research questions,

the researcher must implement the following objectives: (a) gain access to voluntary

participation independent of clinical or industrial "gatekeepers," so as to minimize ethical issues;

(b) profile bullies in a variety of industrial settings identified in the literature as rather more

prone to instances of bullying; (c) tap a sizeable base of respondents and diversity of

organizational environments so as to optimize generalizability (Creswell, 2009) and; (d)

enhance the chances of locating three types of protagonists: perpetrators, victims, and targets

(Matthiesen & Einarsen, 2007).

**Brief Review of the Literature**

**Definitions of Bullying**

Bullying, as opposed to other behaviors, is harder to define. Different scholars and

researches provided a variety of definitions. Griffin and Gross (2004) maintained that bullying is

merely one subset of the entire complex of aggressive behaviors, whether these manifest in the

workplace or earlier, in school. On the other hand, Agervold (2007) described bullying as "a

social interaction through which one individual …is attacked by one or more…individuals

almost on a daily basis and for periods of many months, bringing the person into an almost

helpless position with potentially high risk of expulsion" (p. 162).

Few researchers acknowledged the construct of workplace bullying because the association between bullying and school was so strong (Randle & Stevenson, 2007). The study of bullying in the workplace originated in earlier studies of group-individual dynamics in the workplace. This focused on how cliques and power groups ostracized individuals [who went against norms] by means of ridicule and other behavior (Agervold, 2007). However, different researchers gave the common and essential elements involved in workplace bullying, which involves a perpetrator displaying hostile verbal behavior, coercion, physical contact, and other actions that attack the competence of a colleague at work and degrade the self-esteem of the victim (Forsyth, 2006; Keashly & Jagatic, 2003).

Previous studies also bring the topic more clearly into focus, as most researchers acknowledged that the social circle of the victims or their primary environment is actually the site of bullying. Such observation is found to be much more prevalent than previously thought, causing many companies to develop large-scale prevention programs (Agervold, 2007). While this definition is gaining ground worldwide, United States-based research still folds workplace aggression and incivility into a model to allow for different characterizations of workplace bullying. For instance, according to another definition of bullying, it is seen as " an escalating process in the course of which the person confronted ends up in an inferior position and becomes the target of systematic negative social acts" (Agervold, 2007, p. 16)

Similarly, Agervold (2007) argued that the intention of the bully to harm, and the victim's recognition that harm is intended, is at the core of the concept of bullying. This excludes instances where bully-victims disregard their co-worker's aggressive behavior, thinking it is the latter's normal traits and personality. For this reason, incidents of bullying risk being chronically underreported (Agervold, 2007).

The existence of hidden bullying complicates the research matter. Some forms of bullying barely register to the victim. An instance of this is when an individual's superior has an aggressive management style that would not seem right to be termed or accused as bullying. It becomes bullying only if the individual perceives it as personally directed at him. Because of this ambiguity, the "hazing" culture that new recruits face is not perceived by some as bullying, but as a condition that is common to all recruits "irrespective of how degrading and inhumane it is felt to be" (Agervold, 2007, p. 168). Based on all of these problems, Agervold offered the comprehensive definition that bullying involves regular negative and aggressive communications directed at the self-esteem of the victim, for a period of at least six months, utilizing a temporal threshold to distinguish aggression of a more episodic character (Agervold, 2007).

To test the validity of this definition, Agervold (2007) surveyed over 3,000 workers at a small rural public authority, state institutions, day-care institutions, and psychiatric wards of hospitals using Einarsen's Negative Acts Questionnaire (Agervold, 2007). The results showed varying levels of definitions of bullying. Moreover, as some victims have witnessed other acts of bullying, this weakens the objectivity of their observations. The fact that victims experienced a high degree of stress also exposes reports to bias. Overall, 1% of the subjects reported being bullied, while 4.7% were only exposed to acts of bullying. In over three months, the incidence of bullying acts in these settings was 3.3% (Agervold, 2007).

**Workplace Bullying**

Workplace bullying may include both direct and indirect actions, ranging from verbal abuse to gossip. Bullying can also take the form of personal-related abuse such as questioning a person's mental fitness, to work-related abuse including giving a person too few, too simple, or too many and too difficult tasks to do. Bullying is only believed to happen if an imbalance of power between the persons involved exists, and if it tends "to drain the coping resources of the target, thus in itself emphasizing the increasing powerlessness of targets" (Einarsen et al.,2009, p. 26).

The Einarsen's Negative Acts Questionnaire is an accurate tool in measuring the incidence of workplace bullying, particularly in assessing the degree to which individuals at work are exposed to personal, work-related, and physically intimidating forms of bullying (Einarsen, Hoel & Notelaers, 2009). The scale is built on the theoretical notion that bullying goes beyond discrete events of unpleasantness and entails an often evolving and escalating hostile workplace. This questionnaire also involves both objective measures of bullying and subjective responses by the victims.

Zapf and Einarsen (2003) point to a third set of factors they refer to as "micro political behavior" (p. 10). However, this seems more like an exogenous stimulus in a stressful work environment and therefore opens another direction for inquiry into the effect of leadership styles, particularly as this neglect the need for team structure and well-defined responsibilities (Zapf & Einarsen, 2003).

Emotional abuse, arising from low frustration threshold and a propensity for lashing out, is a frequent manifestation of workplace bullying (Geffner, Braverman, Galasso, & Marsh, 2005). A 1994 survey by the Staffordshire University Business School estimated that no less than half of UK employees were victimized at least once throughout their working life (as cited in Ellis, n.d.). More recent work in the field suggests that bullying may affect as much as 75% of American workers, either as targets or witnesses (Fisher-Blando, 2008).

### Research Method

The mixed methods design is chosen for this research since it the appropriate method to assess the research questions and objectives. In this case, the independent variables include abuse in early childhood, childrearing that condoned physically aggressive behavior, and a single-parent household. The primary dependent variable is defined as either (or both) verbal and physical intimidation that is repetitive and sustained over a period of at least six months and even years. Essential elements are hostility, coercion, and at the extreme, threatened or actual physical contact. A secondary dependent variable is the incidence of bullying or provocative-victim behavior over time frames ranging from the recent past to the entire career span of an employee. In addition, the study will relate the dependent variables to demographic variables, which may provide further delineation to the explanation of the phenomenon. These include: (a) age, (b) income status, (c) educational attainment, (d) industry type, and (e) rank in the organization.

To operationalize the dependent variable, both subjective and frequency-time-based parameters must be incorporated in addition to the verbal and physical manifestations of bullying. The subjective parameters are the participants' perceptions about exposure to negative behavior at work. Meanwhile, the frequency-time-based parameter will be used to compute the actual number of times the victims experience bullying (e.g., once a day, three to five times a week, once a month).

In this study, mixed methods are very likely to involve a planned sequence of research investigations such as, in-depth interviews and survey method. This will begin from drawing out multiple samples of workers from different work settings such as, profit and non-profit businesses. As recommended in the literature, this study will also employ a narrative inquiry in which participants will examine personal experiences of bullying in order to make sense of them. This will be done through in-depth face-to-face interviews. The said approach is appropriate in understanding the perpetuation of bullying in the workplace through the accounts of both the perpetrators and bully-victims.

The qualitative component of the mixed methods research design will address the gaps of previous studies, provide deeper understanding of the complex concept of bullying in the workplace, and confirm if these insights support the quantitative findings in the past researches. Since most applied researches in the past used purely quantitative techniques, the application of qualitative method in this study will be helpful in adding new knowledge to the relatively sparse information about personality traits and family backgrounds of the bullies and their victims.

**Informed Consent**

The researcher will obtain an informed consent from all participants. This will protect their anonymity and the confidentiality of their cases throughout the conduct of the study. This research involves no more than minimal risk of harm or discomfort to all participants, and guarantees that all information would only be used for the purposes of this study.

Before beginning the data collection procedure, participants will read and sign an informed consent letter that explains the purpose of the study and the estimated time of the interview. This letter would reiterate that participation is voluntary and that they can opt out whenever they feel like it. They will have the assurance of the confidentiality of their responses, such that all of the results will only be published in aggregate. Only after accepting the consent and stating that he or she is 18 years of age or older, as well as participating in voluntary basis, will the individual participate in the interview.

Assurances of protection and anonymity will be reiterated during the telephone recruitment of identified bullies or victims for the in-depth interviews. When participants finally meet the researcher in the appointed venue, they will be informed about the expected coverage of the interview such as, the topic of inquiry and the type of questions that would be asked. Trust must be built up else the selected participant has no incentive to divulge intensely private matters about their upbringing, domestic situation, personal traits, lived experience of bullying, and the antecedents of how they learned/adapted to work with others in such a manner.

## Confidentiality

The researcher shall adhere to the confidentiality of all materials gathered during the study. No identifying information shall be attached to any material or information acquired from the participants.

Protecting the anonymity of the respondents in the survey will be achieved by asking them to complete and sign a confidentiality agreement explaining the purpose of the research. This will also express their willingness to participate in the study before the subsequent interviews. The interviews will be tape-recorded upon the consent of the participants. The participants will remain anonymous all throughout the study. Their names will be kept secure and separate from the other demographic data. Furthermore, their names will not be included in the summary report. The people involved in the data analysis (i.e., data gatherer, transcriber, data analyst) will also sign a confidentiality agreement. Therefore, the raw data will not be shared with other participants or persons outside of the project. The data will be stored in a locked filing cabinet in which the researcher would be the only individual with access. By doing this, the confidentiality of each participant in the study will be maintained. After publication, all information directly identifying the study participants shall be removed, so the data can still be used for future research.

## Geographic Location

Even the briefest scan of the literature demonstrates that bullying has been found in a variety of blue-collar and white-collar work settings. More specifically, there is empirical support for bullying in primary health care and academic environments. Given that these work settings have been extensively covered in the literature, the study will cover both profit and non-profit businesses and organizations by arranging anonymous surveys within two counties: Fort Lauderdale and Miami-Dade County in the state of Florida.

**Data Collection Procedures**

To increase the chances of return rates that will satisfy normality assumptions in data analysis later on, the initial survey will extract respondents by cluster sampling and systematic random selection from within the city. Using these procedures will yield an equal probability of selection. As previous researchers employed, this study will use G-power software to determine exact needed sample size. The total sample will depend on the population of Fort Lauderdale and Miami-Dade county areas. The first step in cluster sampling is to divide the population into cluster units. Within these cluster units, the researcher will randomly choose areas where the survey will be conducted. This method will save traveling time and consequently reduce cost. After cluster sampling, each respondent will be systematically chosen by dividing the number of households within the cluster unit by the desired number of respondents (e.g. 150 households/ 25 respondents is equal to six intervals). That will be the interval count in randomly selecting survey respondents. The data gatherer will conduct the survey and give the self-administered questionnaires to the prospective respondents. Each survey will take 15-30 minutes to finish.

Following analysis of the survey results, participants identified as either perpetrators or victims shall be systematically selected for a subsequent interview. The systematic selection will be based on the total sample divided by the number of participants needed for the interview. Here, the line of questioning will focus on their characteristics and behavior with respect to bullying. Branch, Ramsay, and Barker (2007) found that a psychometrics-by-qualitative-interview is entirely applicable for this type of research. These questions aim to discover the characteristics and behavior of bullies, albeit in the case of upward bullying (see definition of terms).

For face validity, the in-depth interviews will open with general questions about satisfaction with career, work environment, leadership styles, and personal strengths and weaknesses. Then, the interview will proceed to probing about experiences with bullying others in the past six months to one year. The interview will indirectly elicit incidence and frequency of bullying behavior by asking what attitudes and actions of colleagues or subordinates provoke one to deal harshly and repeatedly with them. Probes can take the form of asking whether the perpetrator or victim's actions are reasonable; what personal traits of theirs enable respondents to explicitly "tell off" others, and not habitually withdraw from a confrontation; whether these (behaviors) are essential to success in climbing the corporate ladder; how the employee would describe his upbringing and current home life, and so forth.

Owing to the descriptive nature of the study and carefully-neutral construction of the open-ended questions, one need not fear that respondents will simply play back what they hear from the researcher. Rather, this is qualitative inquiry in all its depth, richness, and detail (Schram, 2005; Shank, 2005). Video recording is not an option due to the need to protect the identity of bullying perpetrators. The need for them to remain solely anonymous calls for dual-judge manual coding augmented by computer-aided coding programs like General Inquirer or TextPack (Content-analysis.de, 2009).

**Instrumentation**

The principal survey instrument shall be the Workplace Aggression Research Questionnaire (WARQ) developed by researchers at Wayne State University. WARQ inventories thirty-three instances of hostile, aggressive, and bullying behavior (Keashly & Neuman, 2008). Consistent with the frequency criterion, WARQ instructs respondents to check off only those negative behaviors that they either engage in "regularly" or to which they are subjected intermittently. To operationalize the regularity and frequency of bullying experience, the actual number of reported acts shall be incorporated in the questionnaire. These are: (1) always represents one to five times a day; (2) sometimes represents once a week; (3) rarely represents once a month; and, (4) never.

A vital adjunct to the above questionnaire (and part of the postal survey package) is a heuristically devised scale for all those who experienced being either perpetrators, or victims. Besides querying both groups about their personal characteristics, the scale will inventory their separate child-rearing and family environments so that discriminate analysis may test for any significant differences with respect to experiences of abuse, parenting style, and family structure (i.e., marital, single-parent, other type homes). A sample will be drawn from participants anonymously who admit that they engage in at least one-third of the instances of hostile, aggressive, and bullying behavior measured by either the WARQ or acknowledges having "been the perpetrator myself" in the accompanying Workplace Bullying Institute checklist.

**Validity and Reliability**

External validity is not a strong suite of qualitative interviews. One way to show that the instrument is valid is by showing the face validity of the instrument. The face validity of an instrument "is the degree to which a measure appears to be related to a specific construct" (Furr & Bacharach, 2008, p. 18). This means that the basis for the face validity of the survey instrument used in the proposed study will be how well the items appear to measure the satisfaction of the participants.  Other possible validation methods include the use of convergent

validity, discriminant validity, or construct validity.

The reliability of the instrument will also be assessed.  The reliability indicates that the

items on the survey are internally consistent measurements of the construct in question.  This is

usually determined by calculating Cronbach's alpha coefficients.  Cronbach's alpha coefficients

are used to assess the internal consistency of a group of items used to measure a single construct

(Salkind, 2006).  In general, Cronbach's alpha coefficients range from a low of 0 to a high of 1

with a coefficient of 1 indicating perfect reliability.  A Cronbach's alpha of .70 is considered an

adequate reliability score, and a Cronbach's alpha of .80 is considered a good reliability score

(Salkind, 2006).

Moreover, to ensure reliability, the researcher will personally conduct all in-depth

interviews to minimize the personality of the interviewer as a source of variance.  The level of

variance will increase if other interviewers would be involved in the process (Golafshani, 2003).

**Data Analysis Procedures**

For the qualitative data, NVivo software (Welsh, 2001), a computerized qualitative data

analysis will be used.  The software will provide a means for the researcher to assumedly

distance self from the data and access coding features to detect potential themes and patterns that

emerged.  However, the software cannot guarantee that the researcher will be free of bias.  The

automated tools of the NVivo software application will be useful in analyzing the comprehensive

range of information across diverse sources.  Oswell (2005) posited "the explicit detailed

analysis this software provides add to the overall study's validity and reliability" (p. 89).  The

researcher will therefore analyze and interpret the qualitative data based on the themes and

patterns that emerged from the software.  The expected traits of assertiveness, aggression, hostility, egocentricity, and competitiveness, as obtained by Seign, Coyne, Randal, and Parker (2007), will also be elaborated in this study using the emerging themes and patterns from the data. Researchers deal with the preexisting and naturally occurring phenomena of enduring predispositions that the mere presence or involvement of the researcher does not necessarily incite or exacerbate (Patton, 2002). Still, the researcher will maintain a neutral, accepting stance lest participants become inhibited about admitting to the "anti-social" inclinations of aggression and bullying.

For the quantitative data, the researcher will use both univariate and multivariate analyses. For the univariate analysis of independent variables, frequency tables, percentages, and measures of central tendency (i.e., mean, median, mode) will be used. Mean will be employed for the interval-ratio variables, median for ordinal level variables, and mode for nominal level variables. To determine the relationship between the dependent and independent variables cross tabulation statistical technique with chi-square analysis will be used. The researcher will also use cross tabulation to compare the mean differences of the dependent variables such as age, income status, educational attainment, industry type, and rank in the organization.

**Summary**

The current study aims to better understand the phenomenon of bullying in the workplace. While several studies in the past have empirically reported cases of bullying, most of them have limited coverage using comparatively small samples and non-probability sampling scheme. This research aims to approach the study of bullying using a mixed method design. The use of survey method, in-depth interviews, and heuristically devised scale will give a more comprehensive analysis and interpretation of the topic which will confirm and add to the findings of previous researches. The research design of this study is to inventory a small, yet highly diverse part of a large metropolitan area in the southern United States, adding valuable insights about workplace relationships. The quantitative aspect of this research will indicate the statistical relationships between dependent and independent variables. Meanwhile, the qualitative component of the proposed mixed method approach is central in understanding the characteristics of bully perpetrators and their victims, providing perceptions and detailed description of their self-concept, antecedents, organizational, and family environment. Extant studies reveal a dearth of such diagnostic insights into bullying behavior in the American workplace setting.

References

Adams, A. (1992). *Bullying at work- how to confront and overcome it.* London: Virago.

Agervold, M. (2007). Bullying at work: a discussion of definitions and prevalence, based on an empirical study. *Scandinavian Journal of Psychology, 48,* 161-172. doi: 10.1111/j.1467-9450.2007.00585.x

Anderson C. A. & Bushman, B. J. (2002, February). Human aggression. *Annual Review of Psychology, 53,* 27-51. doi: 10.1146/annurev.psych.53.100901.135231

Atkinson, W. (2000). The everyday face of workplace violence. *Risk Management, 47*(2), 12-18.

Baillien, E., Neyens, I., De Witte, H. & De Cuyper, N. (2009). A qualitative study on the development of workplace bullying: towards a three way model. *Journal of Community & Applied Social Psychology, 19,* 1-16. doi: 10.1002/casp.977

Bing, S. (1992). *Crazy bosses: spotting them, serving them, surviving them.* New York: William Morrow.

Branch, S., Ramsay, S. & Barker, M. (2007). Managers in the firing line: contributing factors to workplace bullying by staff - an interview study. *Journal of Management and Organization, 13*(3), 264-81.

Content-Analysis.de (2009). *Resources related to content analysis and text analysis.* Retrieved from http://www.content-analysis.de/software/quantitative-analysis

Coyne, I., Chong, P. S. L., Seigne, E., & Randall, P. (2003). Self and peer nominations of bullying: An analysis of incident rates, individual differences, and perceptions of the working environment. *European Journal of Work and Organizational Psychology, 12*(3), 209-228.

Creswell, J. W. (2009). *Research design: Qualitative, quantitative, and mixed methods approaches* (3rd ed.). Thousand Oaks, CA: Sage Publications.

Ellis, A. (n.d.). Bullying in the workplace - An acceptable cost? Retrieved from

http://www.workplacebullying.co.uk/aethesis.html.

Einarsen, S. (2000). Harassment and bullying at work: A review of the Scandinavian approach.

*Aggression and Violent Behavior, 4*(5), 379-401.

Einarsen, S., Hoel, H. & Notelaers, G. (2009). Measuring exposure to bullying and harassment at

work: validity, factor structure and psychometric properties of the Negative Acts

Questionnaire-revised. *Work & Stress, 23,* 24-44. doi:10.1080/02678370902815673

Fisher-Blando, J. L. (2008). *Workplace bullying: aggressive behavior and its effect on job*

*satisfaction and productivity.* (Doctoral dissertation, University of Phoenix, 2001).

Forsyth, D. R. (2006). *Group dynamics* (4th ed.). Belmont, CA: Thomson Wadsworth.

Geffner, R., Braverman, M., Galasso, J. & Marsh, J. (Eds.) (2005). *Aggression in organizations:*

*violence, abuse, and harassment at work and in schools.* New York: Routledge.

Giorgi, G. (2009). Workplace bullying risk assessment in 12 Italian organizations. *International*

*Journal of Workplace Health Management, 2* (1), 34–47.

Golafshani, N. (2003). Understanding reliability and validity in qualitative research. *The*

*Qualitative Report, 8*(4), 597-607.

Griffin, R. S., & Gross, A. M. (2004). Childhood bullying: Current empirical findings and future

directions for research. *Aggression and Violent Behavior, 9,* 379-400.

Hoel, H., & Cooper, C. L. (2000). *Destructive conflict and bullying at work.* Manchester, UK:

Manchester School of Management.

Keashly, L., & Jagatic, K. (2003). By another name: American perspectives on workplace

bullying. In S. Einarsen, H. Hoel, D. Zapf, & C. L. Cooper (Eds.), *Bullying and emotional abuse in the workplace* (pp. 31-61). London: Taylor & Francis.

Keashly, L., & Neuman, J. H. (2008). Aggression at the service delivery interface: Do you see what I see? *Journal of Management and Organization, 14*, 180-192.

Kile, S. (1990). Helsefarlige ledere og medarbeidere [Health-dangerous leaders and their co-workers]. Oslo: Hjemmets bokforlag. (qtd. in) Matthiesen, S. B., & Einarsen, S. (2007). Perpetrators and targets of bullying at work: Role stress and individual differences. *Violence and Victims, 22*(6) 735-756.

Matthiesen, S. B., & Einarsen, S. (2007). Perpetrators and targets of bullying at work: Role stress and individual differences. *Violence and Victims, 22*(6), 735-756.

Mikkelsen, E. G., & Einarsen, S. (2001). Bullying in Danish work-life: Prevalence and health correlates. *European Journal of Work and Organizational Psychology, 10*(4), 393-413.

Office for Victims of Crime (2002). *Statistical overview resource guide.* Office of Justice Programs, Department of Justice. Retrieved from http://ojp.usdoj.gov/ovc/ncvrw/2002/pdftxt/statisticaloverview.txt

Patton, M. Q. (2002). *Qualitative research and evaluation methods* (3rd ed.) London: Sage.

Randle, J., & Stevenson, K., (2007). Reducing workplace bullying in healthcare organizations. (Cover story). *Nursing Standard, 21*(22), 49-56.

Schram, T. H. (2005). *Conceptualizing and proposing qualitative research.* Upper Saddle River (NJ): Pearson Merrill Prentice Hall.

Seigne, E., Coyne, I., Randall, P. & Parker, J. (2007). Personality traits of bullies as a contributory factor in workplace bullying: an exploratory study. *International Journal of Organization Theory and Behavior, 10*(1), 118-132.

Shank, G. D. (2005). *Qualitative research: a personal skills approach* (2nd ed.). Upper Saddle

River, NJ: Prentice Hall.

Trochim, W., & Donnelly, J. (2008). *The research methods knowledge base* (3rd ed.). Mason,

OH: Cengage.

Vartia, M. (1996). The sources of bullying-Psychological work environment and organizational

climate. *European Journal of Work and Organizational Psychology, 5*, 203-205.

Workplace Bullying Institute (2007). *Results of the WBI U.S. workplace bullying survey.*

Retrieved from http://www.workplacebullying.org/research/furtherstudies.html

Zapf, D., & Einarsen, S. (2003). Individual antecedents of bullying. In S. Einarsen, H. Yildiz, S.

(2007). A 'new' problem in the workplace: psychological abuse (bullying). *Akademik*

*Arastirmalar Dergisi, 34,* 113-128.

**Appendix**

Harvey, M.G., Heames, J. T., Richey, R. G., & Leonard, N. (2006).  Bullying: From the

playground to the boardroom. *Journal of Leadership & Organizational Studies, 12*, 1-11.

This study examined three components of bullying: The organizational environment,

characteristics of bullies, and characteristics of those who are bullied.  Using research rather

than firsthand studies to support their ideas, the authors contend that the combination of the

tendency for childhood bullies to mature into bullying adults combined with an increasingly

stressful global business environment, increases the possibility of incidences of workplace

bullying.  They also concluded that since bullying is a part of human nature that do not seem

to be going away any time soon, it is up to organizational leaders to assess their

organization's environment to address the issue.

Lampman, C., Phelps, A., Bancroft, S., & Beneke, A. (2009).  Contrapower harassment in

academia: A survey of faculty experience with student incivility, bullying, and sexual

attention. *Sex Roles, 60(5)*. 331-346.

In this article, the authors discussed contra power harassment, which was as "a situation

where a person with lesser power within an institution harasses an individual with greater

power." Using a sample of Alaskan college professors, the authors conducted a survey about

their experiences with such harassment from students.  Out of all faculty members surveyed

(N=654), about half returned the survey (N = 399). The response rate for men (63%) and

women (61%) was similar.  Using a principal components factor analysis on 30 student

behavior items, the authors found that the majority of faculty members, both male and

female, faculty experienced student harassment.  For example, the first factor measured on a

scale labeled "incivility-bullying," the scores ranged from 1.00 to 3.67.

Pollak, S. D., Vardi, S., Putzer Bechner, A.M., & Curtin, J. J. (2005). Physically abused

children's regulation of attention in response to hostility. *Journal of Child Development, 76,*

968-977.

Pollak, Vardi, Putzer Bechner, and Curtin (2005) measured a small group of eleven abused

children's (N=11) reactions to the unfolding of a realistic interpersonal emotional situation

through multiple methods including autonomic nervous system changes and overt behavioral

performance. Using electrodes on the children's arms and legs to measure emotional arousal,

as well as observation of behavior, they found that although physically abused and non-

physically abused 4-year-old children did not differ in terms of their baseline levels of

arousal, there were differences in physically abused children's regulatory responses to

background anger emerged. Separate "within-period" analyses were conducted for heart rate

(HR) and skin conductance level (SCL) within each of the three target periods (active anger,

unresolved anger, and resolution). For each measure and period, a multivariate repeated

measures ANOVA was conducted. A one-sample t-test determined that the overall HR

deceleration observed throughout the active anger period for both groups (M = -2.0) was

significant, t (31)-4.24, p<. 001. For SCL, a significant Group X quadratic Time interaction

was observed during the active anger period (F(1,30)= 4.22, P=.05). A Continuous

Performance Test (CPT) was also administered to measure performance and each analyzed,

separated within multivariate repeated measures ANOVAs, with significant effect of age

covariates for both response time (F(1,30) = 10.22, P = .003) and memory (F(1.29 – 4.93,

P=.05).The acknowledged limitations of the study include the small sample size, the

imprecise nature of the electrode data, and the fact that the stimuli the researchers used were

not always relevant to the children's backgrounds and concerns. Despite these limitations, these data suggest that the emergence of anger leads to increases in anticipatory monitoring

of the environment among children with histories of abuse.

Conger, R. D., Neppl, T., Jeong Kim, K., & Scaramella, L. (2003). Angry and aggressive

behavior across three generations: A prospective, longitudinal study of parents and children.

*Journal of Abnormal Child Psychology, 31*, 143.

This longitudinal design study is both observational and measures using multiple informants

to prove it. The researchers interviewed their subjects on an annual basis for about ten years.

This allowed them to overcome some of the methodological limitations that occurred in

earlier research on multigenerational transmission of aggression. One of the study's main

strengths is the direct observation of interactions between parents and children. Data was

collected from second-generation youth (G2), their mothers (G1), and their children (G3).

They also used a large sample of 558 young people (N = 558) and their families, including

younger siblings. However, the study did have some limitations, such as the relatively short

duration of the observational tasks. The authors also relied on the assumption of a common

element of stress for family members even though the interaction tasks involved different

people and situations.

Curtner-Smith, M. E., Culp, A.M., Culp, R., Scheib, C., Owen, K., Tilley, A., Murphy, M., &

Coleman, P. W. (2006). Mother's parenting and young economically disadvantaged

children's relational and overt bullying. *Journal of Child and Family Studies, 15*, 181-193.

This article examined the relationship between mothers' parenting and children's

bullying using a sample of children in a Head Start program. They conducted face-to- face

interviews with the mothers and also had them fill out surveys. They began their report by

citing a Canadian study that revealed, among other things, that boys who demonstrated the most aggressive behavior at age 6 were more likely to continue exhibiting physically

aggressive behavior throughout childhood and adolescence (p. 182). They also

distinguished between physical or overt bullying and relational bullying, which relies more

on verbal assault, social exclusion, and other forms of humiliation. This is an important

distinction because, just as emotional abuse in a relationship can be just as damaging as

physical abuse, bullying does not always have to be physical in nature to cause significant

emotional and psychological damage to the victim.

In terms of methodology, the authors used a sample of 44 mothers and their children (both

male and female), most of whom were African-American (mean children = 4.11 SD = 64).

Gender distribution for children was 64% female and 34 % male. The authors had the

teachers complete the Preschool Social Behavior Scale-Teacher (PSBS-T) for each child,

with options ranging from "Almost never true" to "Almost always true." Scores ranged

from 6 to 25, (M = 10.82; SD = 5.0) Chrombach alpha - .93. Using a combination of

parental self-reporting and teacher reports of the children's behavior, the authors concluded

that their findings were consistent with those of other studies, and that maternal parenting

and expectations did have an effect on the level of aggression the children showed. While

focusing on children from low-income households seems a bit limiting, the authors highlight

that as a potential factor, noting that these children were at a higher risk due to lack of

cognitive stimulation, harsh parental discipline, and other factors related to low income

families. This was a valid point, and relevant to many school and work environments.

However, bullying is hardly limited to this group, and it should be acknowledged that other

factors might be involved. More research is needed on bullying among children of all socio-

economic backgrounds.

School bullies turn into 'bad parents'. (2006, July 12). Irish Independent. Retrieved January 8,

　　　2011, from ProQuest Newsstand. (Document ID: 1075952961).

　　　This article from the Irish Independent (2006) featured a report of a long-term study of

　　　children and their parents that led to the expected conclusion about the transference of violent

　　　behavior from parents to children. It is included　the population sample was taken from a

　　　different culture than of many studies done in the United States, and it also contributes

　　　evidence to support this writer's findings on this topic.

Ayoko, Q. B. (2007). Communication openness, conflict events and reactions to conflict in

　　　culturally diverse workgroups/ cross-cultural management: *International Journal, 14,*105-

　　　124.

　　　This research study focused on social identity theory using current research as a framework

　　　regarding relationships between variables and bullying in the workplace. The strength of

　　　this approach is that it allowed Ayoko to examine bullying quantitatively in workgroup

　　　settings (one of the few studies to do so) and to examine how openness of communication

　　　affects workplace bullying and the emotional reaction to it in a broader way than a single

　　　study may have done. There were multiple weakness to this study: (a) it focused mostly on

　　　cultural diversity, (b) other potential relevant factors such as age gender were not controlled

　　　for in the analysis, and (c) the potential impact of age and gender were not given enough

　　　consideration. However, the highlighting of communication in the workplace was important

　　　both in the understanding of and preventing incidences of such behavior, which could help

　　　managers, confront the issue more knowledgeably.

Glendinning, P.M. (2001). Workplace bullying: Curing the cancer of the American workplace.

　　　*Journal of Public Personnel Management 30,* 269-286.

Glendinning (2001) examined the results on an extensive literature review in which he

examined the hypothesis that bullying of employees by supervisors is an increasingly

important issue in the modern workplace due to the tight labor market (at the time the article

was written). Glendinning, identified what motivates employees to quit their jobs 95% said

"whether or not they will be able to develop a trusting relationship with their manager.

Additionally, what motivates supervisors to bully and the types of organizations that foster

bullying behaviors. It was concluded that workplace bullying is a real, widespread

phenomenon with high costs to both the employee and the organization. The main

proposition was that employees would not tolerate such behavior. It would be interesting to

see a similar study conducted in the current economic environment.

Roscigno, V., Lopez, S. & Hodson, R. (2009). Supervisory bullying: Status inequalities and

organizational context. *Journal of Social Forces, 87*, 1561-1589.

In this highly technical article, the authors reported the results of complex multi-method

analyses of organizational attributes that contribute to workplace bullying. They took data

from the population of "book length organizational ethnographies." The cohort (N = 204)

was selected from a variety of businesses that recently published new or updated

ethnographies. The authors' in this study contended that sexual harassment is a type of

bullying. Social class and job insecurity can make some workers more vulnerable to

workplace bullying, and that bullying may be more frequent "in workplaces with direct

personal supervision and/or chaotic procedures and organization." Guardians such as

police, trade unions, and family members can protect potential victims. The authors

concluded "Organizational responses to bullying need to move beyond a Band-aid approach

in which each incident is handled individually.

Salin, D. (2003). Review of enabling, motivating, and precipitating structures and processes in

    the work environment. *Journal of Human Relations 56,* 1213.

    Salin (2003) focused on the literature for workplace bullying and, like Said, indicated

    that it would continue to have serious consequences in society. He used the literature to

    support his assertion that factors such as perceived power imbalance could create dangerous

    conditions in the workplace if they are not addressed skillfully. Although it does not have

    the immediacy of a study actually conducted by the author, such thorough research studies

    are very useful in putting the vast amount of research into perspective.

Djurkovic, N., McCormack, D., & Casimir, G. (2006). Neuroticism and the psychosomatic

    model of workplace bullying. *Journal of Managerial Psychology, 21(1/2),* 73-88. Retrieved

    June 21, 2009, from ABI/INFORM Global database. (Document ID: 1024161871).

This study used a survey approach to determine whether the negative effects of bullying were

independent of, or is moderated by, neuroticism. Although this may seem like too fine a point

to make much difference, it is a valuable distinction  because it can shed light on whether

people who suffer psychological effects from bullying are physiologically and

psychologically predisposed to such reactions. Some of the limitations of this study includes:

(a) a small sample,  (b) self-reporting, and (c) cross-sectional data, If these findings were

expanded, they may have strong implications for employers and managers who may be held

accountable for preventing this behavior  to occur.

Matthiesen, S. B., & Einarsen., S. (2007).  Perpetrators and targets of bullying at work: Role

    stress and individual differences. *Journal of Violence and Victims, 22,* 735-756.

    Matthiesen and Einarsen (2007) also used a survey format; in this case to determine whether

    bullies and their victims were under similar workplace stress before bullying incidents occur.

Of the sample (N = 2215), 47% responded; 3.4% could be categorized as perpetrators, 2.1%

provocative victims, and 8.3% as targets of bullying. In addition, 53% were men and 47%

were women, the sample size of 4,742 labor union members is large enough for the results to

have good transferability, and they represent a good variety of fields. However, the authors

acknowledged that a limitation in their method was that participants were asked about

sensitive subjects and may not have answered with complete honesty. They also

acknowledged "measurement of perpetrator behavior is methodologically difficult." This is

a common difficulty of behavioral studies in general, and emphasizes the need to conduct

them with great care and to not jump to conclusions.

Thomas, M. (2005). Bullying among support staff in a higher education institution. *Journal of*

*Health Education, 105*, 273-286.

The researcher conducted on a small, exploratory study to examine support staff   perceptions

of the nature and causes of bullying and the perceived relationship between bullying and self-

reported health complaints. The author distributed self-report questionnaires and conducted

interviews with participants who felt that they were victims of bullying to expand on the data

from the questionnaires. From a total of 42 respondents (N= 42), 19 reported experiencing one

or more forms of bullying in the previous two years, and 17 had witnessed colleagues being

bullied. Headaches, fatigue, and stomach and bowel problems were the most commonly

reported physical ailments. The author acknowledged, "Generalizability is compromised as

very specific data was collected from a particular group of people." Other limitations included

that the subjects were not randomly selected but volunteered to participate in the study

themselves, and that the staff of the organization in the study was predominantly female.

Trotter, J. L. & Allen, N. E. (2009). The good, the bad, and the ugly: Domestic violence survivors' experiences with their informal social networks. *AM J Community*

*Psychology, 43*,221-231. Department of Psychology, University of Illinois.

Trotter and Allen (2009) conducted a qualitative research study to examine the range of

possible reactions survivors of domestic abuse may encounter from their social networks.

They begun by discussing previous research on the affects of social support on victims of

domestic violence as well as the difficulty of defining social support and explain how

they examined it mainly in terms of the perception of the victims' perceptions of it

(positive, negative, and mixed). Although the sample size is fairly small, the authors'

findings are hard to dispute as they took a very disciplined approach to studying a

complex subject. It is also relevant to my topic since domestic abuse is closely related to

bullying behavior (and in many cases is an extension of it).

Beightol, J., Jevertson, J. Gray, S., Carter, S., & Gass, M. (2008). The effect of an experimental,

adventure-based "anti-bullying initiative" on levels of resilience: A mixed methods study.

State Education & Environmental Roundtable. *Retrieved on from www.seer.org.*

Using a "mixed methods, quasi-experimental design," Beightol, Jevertson, Gray, et. al

(2008) examined the effects of participation in an anti-bullying program in an elementary

school. The program included ten sessions of role-plays and problem solving activities. A

series of nonparametric tests demonstrated that participation I this program did correlate

with enhanced levels of goal and aspirations ($z = -2.581$, $p<.010$, $r=.25$)The study sample

size included 51 students ($n = 51$; male $= 26$, female $= 25$) in the treatment group and 54

students in the comparison group. Results also showed a significant increase in self-

efficacy for the treatment group ( $= -2669$, $p = .008$, $r = .26$). The authors cite "ceiling

effect, abnormal data distributions, and low correlation coefficients" as limitations of the study, the results indicate that participation in such programs may increase children's sense of resilience and thus reduce the negative impact of bullying behavior.

Rozensky, R. H., N. G. Johnson, C. D., Goodheart, & R. H., Hammond (2003). *Psychology Builds a Healthy World: Opportunities for Research and Practice.* Washington DC: American Psychological Association.

This book review used an anecdotal approach to support the proposition that family connections are the most important factor in preventing incidences of violent behavior. The researchers were able to catch the reader's attention exploring the actual scope of the problem in vivid detail. The fact that the incidences and their perpetrators were are each unique yet shared common threads strengthened his contention that teen violence does have common causes, and that a common need for stronger family connections may hold the key to preventing such tragedies from happening in the future. This approach may not be purely scientific, but it is very effective in that it addresses a serious social issue in a way anyone can understand.

Said, C. (2007). Bullying bosses could be busted: Movement against worst workplace abusers gains momentum with proposed laws. San Francisco Chronicle. Retrieved on May 7, 2009 from http://www.sfgate.com/cgi-bin/article.cgi? f=/c/a/2007/01/21/ BUG7DNKKN61.DTL.

Said (2007) derive a more contextual and anecdotal approach to the issue, suggesting that legislation may be required due to the seriousness of the issue. However, he does take a balanced look at both sides of the issue, using quotes from those who feel that such legislation would be wrong to those who feel it is inevitable. Such research helps both the researcher and the reader place their own findings and observations in context, and can also highlight important changes in society.

9 783656 259589